Mack and Pip

Written by Caroline Green

Illustrated by Angelika Scudamore

Collins

Mack and Pip pack.

Dad and Nan tip.

Pip is in a sack.

Mack and Nan sit.

Pip is on top!

Dad is in a cap.

Pip and Nan sip.

Mack kicks it in!

Mack got a pin!

Dad and Pip pat Mack.

Pip and Mack nap.

Dad pins it on.

 Review: After reading

Use your assessment from hearing the children read to choose any GPCs, words or tricky words that need additional practice.

Read 1: Decoding

- Reread page 10. Ask the children to point to the word that tells us what Mack gets. (*pin*)
- Reread page 13 and ask the children to point to the word that tells us what Dad does. (*pins*)
- Ask the children to sound out and blend these words:

pack **got** **kicks** **cap**

- Turn to page 2 and say: Read about what Mack and Pip do. Can you blend the words in your head when you read?
  - Repeat for page 3, asking: Read what Dad and Nan do. Again, encourage children to blend the words in their head.

Read 2: Prosody

- Turn to pages 8 and 9.
  - Model reading page 8, reading slowly and emphasising the names and verb. Point out how you are reading slowly to show how Pip and Nan are just resting and having a drink.
  - Model reading page 9, increasing the pace for the excitement of the speed of the action. Discuss why you have read this page faster.
  - Encourage the children to read the same pages, using a slower pace for the sitting and sipping, and a faster pace for Mack kicking the ball in.

Read 3: Comprehension

- Ask the children if they have seen or been in races like Mack and Pip. Ask: What happened?
- Discuss whether Pip and Mack are good at games and sport.
  - Ask the children to look back at the story to find out how well Mack did, and how well Pip did.
  - Discuss their findings and whether they think Mack and Pip were good at sport.
- Turn to pages 12 and 13.
  - Ask: How do you think Mack and Pip feel? Why? (*tired because they have been running around*)
  - Ask: How do you think Dad is feeling? Why? (*proud because Mack and Pip did well*)
- Look at the "I spy sounds" pages (14–15) together. Ask the children to point out as many things that they can in the picture that begin with the /p/ sound. (*Pip, plant, picture, panda, penguin, pins, pineapple, pears, pizza, pens, pen pot, paints, paintbrushes, pans, plates*)